anythink

SHOW ME
GE⊕GRAPHY

WEATHER
AROUND THE WORLD

By
Emilie Dufresne

KidHaven
PUBLISHING

Published in 2022 by
KidHaven Publishing, an Imprint of Greenhaven Publishing, LLC
353 3rd Avenue
Suite 255
New York, NY 10010

© 2022 Booklife Publishing
This edition is published by arrangement with Booklife Publishing

Edited by: Madeline Tyler
Designed by: Gareth Liddington

Cataloging-in-Publication Data

Names: Dufresne, Emilie.
Title: Weather around the world / Emilie Dufresne.
Description: New York : KidHaven Publishing, 2022. | Series: Show me geography | Includes glossary and index.
Identifiers: ISBN 9781534538306 (pbk.) | ISBN 9781534538320 (library bound) | ISBN 9781534538313 (6 pack) | ISBN 9781534538337 (ebook)
Subjects: LCSH: Weather--Juvenile literature. | Meteorology--Juvenile literature. | Climatology--Juvenile literature.
Classification: LCC QC981.3 D843 2022 | DDC 551.5--dc23

Printed in the United States of America

CPSIA compliance information: Batch #CSKH22: For further information contact Greenhaven Publishing LLC, New York, New York at 1-844-317-7404.

Please visit our website, www.greenhavenpublishing.com. For a free color catalog of all our high-quality books, call toll free 1-844-317-7404 or fax 1-844-317-7405.

Find us on

Photo Credits:

4 – angkirt, GenerationClash, 5 – Anna Frajtova, 6 – Maifoxky, peiyang, Artemil Sanin, 7 – MAKSIM ANKUDA, Oleksil Arseniuk, 8 – naum, Pretty Vectors, 9 – Pilvitus, 10 – FANTRAZZY, 11 – Krushevskaya, 12 – Fluke Cha, 14 – Sin314, miniwide, 15 – Maquiladora, BigMouse, 16 – trgrowth, 17 – GraphicsRF, intararit, 18 – TeraVector, NotionPic, 20 – Andramin, RealVector, vladwel.

Images are courtesy of Shutterstock.com. With thanks to Getty Images, Thinkstock Photo, and iStockphoto.

Contents

Words that look like this can be found in the glossary on page 24.

What Is Weather?

Look out of the window – is it sunny, rainy, or cloudy? What temperature is it? Is it hot or cold? Whatever it's like outside, that is the weather!

Here are some types of weather that you might have seen.

Sunny

Snowy

Foggy

Windy

Stormy

Rainy

Cloudy

Cold

Hot

Why Do We Have Weather?

The sun warms up different places on Earth at different times. This means that there is always both warm air and cold air on Earth.

When cold air and warm air meet, clouds, rain, and thunderstorms can be formed.

The weather will be different because of the time of day, season, and place.

In summer, it is usually warmer.

North Pole

In winter, it is usually colder.

Equator

Places near the equator are hotter.

Places that are near the North Pole and South Pole are colder.

South Pole

Forecasting Weather

Special scientists called meteorologists study the weather. This lets them <u>predict</u> what the weather might be like before it happens.

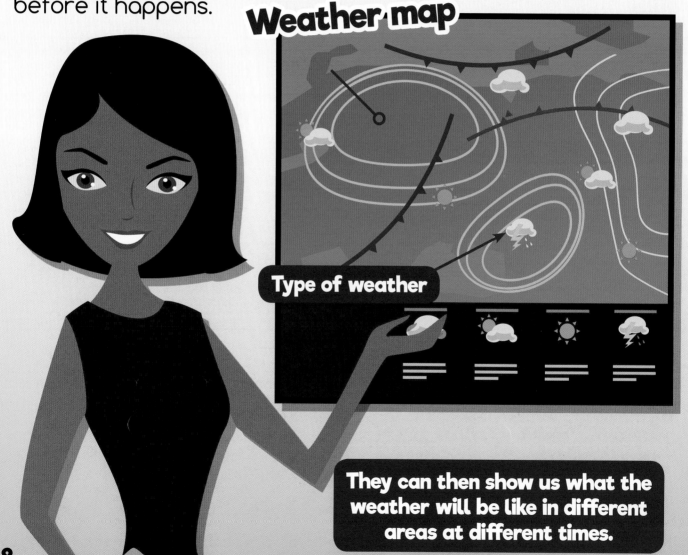

Weather map

Type of weather

They can then show us what the weather will be like in different areas at different times.

Weather maps can be quite confusing, with lots of different <u>symbols</u> on them. As well as the ones on page 5, you might see these symbols during a weather forecast.

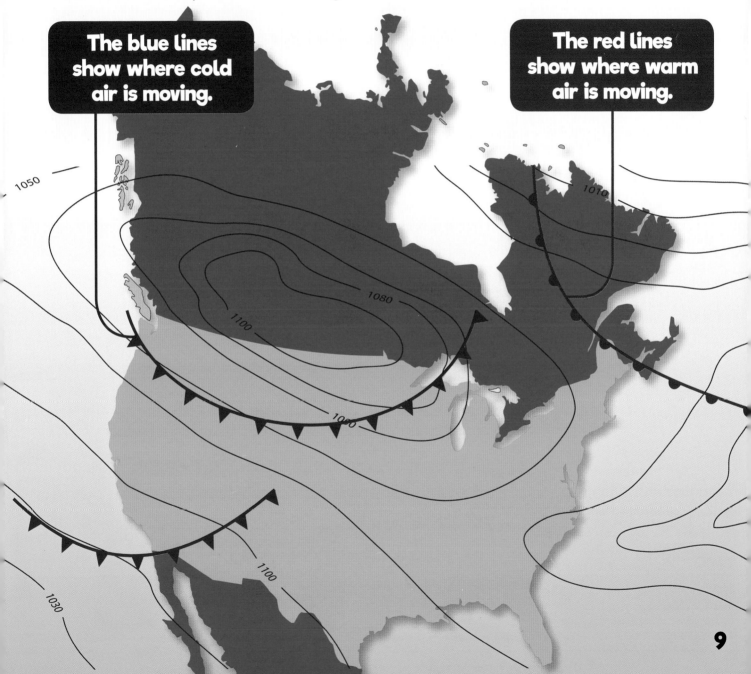

The blue lines show where cold air is moving.

The red lines show where warm air is moving.

Snowflakes

Water droplets in the air usually turn into rain. However, when it is very cold, they can freeze. The frozen water droplets create ice crystals.

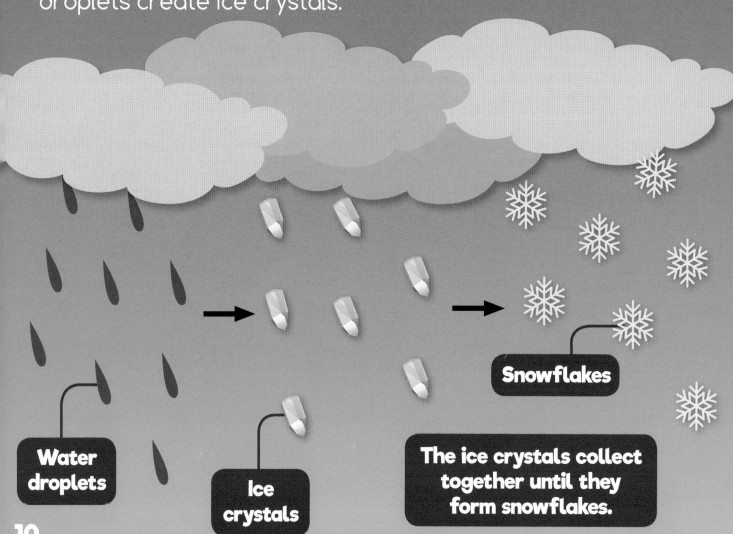

Water droplets

Ice crystals

Snowflakes

The ice crystals collect together until they form snowflakes.

Snowflakes are so small that they all look the same to us. But if you look at them under a microscope, you can see that they are all very different.

Snowflakes can come in all these shapes and more.

Clouds

Clouds are very important. They <u>regulate</u> Earth's temperature and carry rain that is needed for things to grow.

Different types of clouds form at different heights in the sky.

CUMULONIMBUS
These clouds are very large and reach high up, through many layers of the sky.

CIRRUS
These are wispy, thin clouds found high up in the sky. They usually mean a change in weather is coming.

ALTOSTRATUS

These are wide sheets of thin clouds that form in the middle of the sky and don't let much sunlight through.

CUMULUS

Bright white and cauliflower shaped, these clouds usually mean that the weather is sunny.

Animals and Weather

Fennec Fox

Animals can live in lots of different places on Earth. Fennec foxes have <u>adapted</u> to live in very hot areas.

Their large ears keep them cool in the heat.

They sleep underground in dens during the day to keep cool.

Very furry feet stop the hot sand from burning them.

Arctic Fox

Arctic foxes live in one of the coldest places on Earth. Let's take a look at how they have adapted to live in the Arctic.

Their thick, bushy tail helps to keep them warm.

Their small ears and nose stop them from losing heat.

They live in burrows underneath the snow and out of the cold.

Climate Change

Humans are damaging Earth by using lots of <u>fossil fuels</u>. Fossil fuels produce <u>greenhouse gases</u> that trap warm air on Earth.

Greenhouse gases

Trapped warm air

The word "climate" means what the weather is like in one place over a long time.

Drought

As Earth gets warmer and warmer, our climate will start changing. The ice caps will melt and there will be more extreme weather, such as droughts and floods.

Flood

Storm Hunters

Storm hunters have a very important, but scary, job. They take special <u>equipment</u> into the middle of some of the biggest storms in the world.

This equipment helps them to know how and why big storms form.

If scientists or meteorologists know more about how and why big storms form, it will help them to know when a big storm is coming. This would help people stay safe.

Weather Instruments

There are lots of tools that we use to see what the weather is doing. These tools are called instruments. Let's take a look at some of them and what they do.

WEATHER SATELLITES – These study large air movements and storms from space.

ANEMOMETERS – The cups "catch" the wind and tell us how fast the wind is traveling.

WEATHER BALLOONS – These large balloons measure the weather much higher up in the sky.

THERMOMETERS – These tell us how hot or cold a place or thing is.

°F °C

What's That Cloud?

Take a look at these clouds. Can you match each cloud with the right name?

1

2

3

4

Go outside and look at the clouds. What type of clouds do you think they are?

**A. Cumulonimbus B. Cirrus
C. Cumulus D. Altostratus**

Answers: 1C, 2A, 3D, 4B

22

What's the Weather Like?

Look at this picture of Earth.
What signs do you think need to go where?

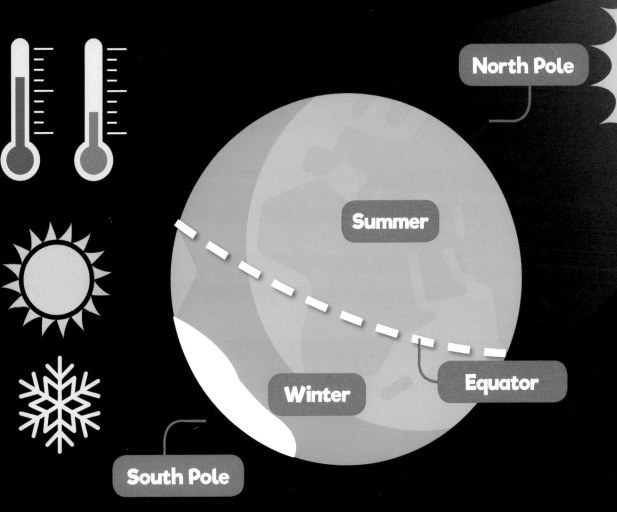

Glossary

adapt	to change over time to suit the environment
drought	a long period of very little rainfall, which can lead to a lack of water
equator	the imaginary line around Earth that is an equal distance from the North and South Poles
equipment	items that are needed to complete a certain job
fossil fuel	a source of energy, such as coal, oil, and gas, that formed millions of years ago from the remains of animals and plants
greenhouse gas	a gas in the air that traps the sun's heat
predict	to guess what will happen in the future
regulate	to keep in a certain way
symbol	an image that represents something else

Index